A s‹

Luke 11, 1.
"Lord teach us to pray, as John taught his disciples."
He said to them, "When you pray, say:

Our Father, who art in heaven,
hallowed be Thy name;
Thy kingdom come;
Thy will be done on earth
as it is in heaven.
Give us this day our daily bread;
And forgive us our trespasses
as we forgive those
who trespass against us;
And lead us not into temptation,
but deliver us from evil." Amen.

Nihil Obstat: George J. Ziskovsky, *Censor Deputatus*
Imprimatur: ✠ Leo C. Byrne
Coadjutor Archbishop of St. Paul and Minneapolis

THE LEAFLET MISSAL COMPANY
976 W. Minnehaha Ave.   St. Paul, Minnesota 55104
Printed in U.S.A

Morning Offering

✠

O Jesus,
   through the Immaculate Heart of Mary, I
   offer You all my prayers, works, and sufferings of this day. For all the intentions of
   Your Sacred Heart. In union with the Holy
   Sacrifice of the Mass throughout the world.
   In reparation for all my sins. For the intentions of all our associates, and, in particular,
   for the intention of our Holy Father for this
   month.   *Amen.*

The Hail Mary

✠

Hail, Mary! Full of grace,
   The Lord is with thee;
   Blessed are thou among women,
   And blessed is the fruit of thy womb, Jesus.
   Holy Mary, Mother of God,
   Pray for us sinners,
   Now, and at the hour of our death.   *Amen.*

Adoration

✠

Glory be to the Father, and to the Son, and to the
   Holy Spirit: As it was in the beginning, is
   now, and ever shall be, world without end.
   Amen.

Apostles' Creed

✠

I believe in God the Father Almighty, Creator
of heaven and earth; and in Jesus Christ,
His only Son, our Lord, Who was conceived
by the Holy Spirit, born of the Virgin Mary,
suffered under Pontius Pilate, was crucified,
died, and was buried.

He descended into hell; the third day He rose
again from the dead.

He ascended into heaven, sitteth at the right hand
of God, the Father Almighty. From thence He
shall come to judge the living and the dead.

I believe in the Holy Spirit, the Holy Catholic
Church, the communion of Saints, the forgiveness of sins, the resurrection of the body,
and life everlasting. *Amen.*

Fruits of the Holy Spirit

Charity, Joy, Peace, Patience, Benignity,
Goodness, Longanimity, Mildness, Faith,
Modesty, Continence, Chastity.

Gifts of the Holy Spirit

Wisdom, Understanding, Counsel, Fortitude,
Knowledge, Piety, Fear of the Lord.

The Beatitudes

✠

Blessed are the poor in spirit,
    for theirs is the kingdom of heaven.

Blessed are the meek,
    for they shall possess the earth.

Blessed are they who mourn,
    for they shall be comforted.

Blessed are they who hunger and thirst for
        justice,
    for they shall be satisfied.

Blessed are the merciful,
    for they shall obtain mercy.

Blessed are the clean of heart,
    for they shall see God.

Blessed are the peacemakers,
    for they shall be called children of God.

Blessed are they who suffer persecution for
        justice' sake,
    for theirs is the kingdom of heaven.

Blessed are you when men reproach you, and
    persecute you, and speaking falsely, say all
    manner of evil against you, for My sake.

The Mysteries of the Rosary

✠

Joyful Mysteries *(Monday and Saturday)*
1. The Annunciation *(Humility)*
2. The Visitation *(Charity)*
3. The Nativity *(Poverty)*
4. The Presentation of the Child Jesus in the Temple *(Obedience)*
5. The Finding of the Child Jesus in the Temple *(Piety)*

The Sorrowful Mysteries *(Tuesday and Friday)*
1. The Agony in the Garden *(Contrition)*
2. The Scourging of Jesus at the Pillar *(Purity)*
3. The Crowning of Jesus with Thorns *(Courage)*
4. The Carrying of the Cross *(Patience)*
5. The Crucifixion and Death of Jesus *(Self-denial)*

The Glorious Mysteries *(Wednesday and Sunday)*
1. The Resurrection of Jesus *(Faith)*
2. The Ascension of Jesus *(Hope)*
3. The Descent of the Holy Spirit *(Love)*
4. The Assumption of Mary into Heaven *(Eternal Happiness)*
5. The Coronation of Mary in Heaven *(Devotion to Mary)*

The Luminous Mysteries *(Thursday)*
1. The Baptism of Jesus in the Jordan *(Repentance)*
2. The Wedding Feast at Cana *(Commitment)*
3. The Kingdom of God *(Evangelization)*
4. The Transfiguration of Jesus *(Perseverance)*
5. The Holy Eucharist *(The Mass)*

The Angelus

V. The Angel of the Lord declared unto Mary,
R. And she conceived of the Holy Spirit.
    Hail Mary, etc.

V. Behold the handmaid of the Lord.
R. Be it done unto me according to Your Word.
    Hail Mary, etc.

V. And the word was made flesh,
R. And dwelt among us.
    Hail Mary, etc.

V. Pray for us O holy Mother of God.
R. That we may be made worthy of the prom-
    ises of Christ.

Let us pray:
Pour forth, we beseech You, O Lord, Your
    Grace into our hearts; that as we have
    known the incarnation of Christ, your Son
    by the message of an angel, so by His pas-
    sion and cross we may be brought to the
    glory of His Resurrection.   Through the
    same Christ, our Lord.   *Amen.*

Mary Mother of Grace

Mary, Mother of grace,
    Mother of mercy,
    Shield me from the enemy
    And receive me at the hour of my death.
    (Roman Ritual)

The Salve Regina
✠

Hail, Holy Queen, Mother of Mercy.

Hail our life, our sweetness and our hope!

To You do we cry, poor banished children of Eve!

To You do we send up our sighs; mourning and
weeping in this vale of tears!

Turn then, most gracious Advocate, Your eyes of
mercy toward us; and after this, our exile,
show unto us the blessed fruit of Your womb,
Jesus!

O clement, O loving, O sweet Virgin Mary!

The Memorare
✠

Remember, O most gracious Virgin Mary that
never was it known that anyone who fled to
your protection, implored your help, or
sought your intercession was left unaided.

Inspired with this confidence, I fly to you O Virgin
of virgins, my mother. To you I come; before
you I stand, sinful and sorrowful.

O Mother of the Word Incarnate, despise not
my petitions, but in your mercy, hear and
answer me. *Amen.*

Magnificat

✠

My soul magnifies the Lord,
   and my spirit rejoices in God my Savior;

Because He has regarded the lowliness of His
handmaid;
   for, behold, henceforth all generations shall
   call me blessed;

Because He who is mighty has done great
things for me,
   and holy is His name;

And His mercy is from generation to generation
   on those who fear Him.

He has shown might with His arm,
   He has scattered the proud in the conceit
   of their heart.

He has put down the mighty from their thrones,
   and has exalted the lowly.

He has filled the hungry with good things,
   and the rich He has sent away empty.

He has given help to Israel, His servant, mindful of His mercy——

Even as He spoke to our fathers——
   to Abraham and to His posterity forever.

Prayer to Saint Joseph
✠

O Blessed Saint Joseph, faithful guardian and protector of virgins, to whom God entrusted Jesus and Mary, I implore you by the love which you did bear them, to preserve me from every defilement of soul and body, that I may always serve them in holiness and purity of love. *Amen.*

Prayer to Christ the King
✠

Christ Jesus, I acknowledge You King of the universe. All that has been created has been made for You. Make full use of Your rights over me.

I renew the promises I made in Baptism, when I renounced Satan and all his pomps and works, and I promise to live a good Christian life and to do all in my power to procure the triumph of the rights of God and Your Church.

Divine Heart of Jesus, I offer You my efforts in order to obtain that all hearts may acknowledge Your Sacred Royalty, and that thus the Kingdom of Your peace may be established throughout the universe. *Amen.*

Prayer of St. Francis of Assisi

✠

Lord, make me an instrument of Your peace.

Where there is hatred, let me sow love;

Where there is injury, pardon;

Where there is doubt, faith;

Where there is despair, hope;

Where there is darkness, light;

And where there is sadness, joy.

O Divine Master, grant that I may not so much seek to be consoled as to console; to be understood as to understand; to be loved as to love. For it is in giving that we receive, it is in pardoning that we are pardoned, and it is in dying that we are born to eternal life.

Prayer for Priests

✠

O Jesus, I pray for Your faithful and fervent priests; for Your unfaithful and tepid priests; for Your priests laboring at home or abroad in distant mission fields; for Your tempted priests; for Your lonely and desolate priests; for Your young priests; for Your dying priests; for the souls of Your priests in purgatory.

But above all I recommend to You the priests dearest to me; the priest who baptized me; the priests who absolved me from my sins; the priests at whose Masses I assisted and who gave me Your Body and Blood in Holy Communion; the priests who taught and instructed me; all the priests to whom I am indebted in any other way. O Jesus, keep them all close to Your heart, and bless them abundantly in time and in eternity. *Amen.*

Prayer in Time of Sickness

✠

O Jesus, You suffered and died for us;

You understand suffering;

Teach me to understand my suffering as You do;

To bear it in union with You;

To offer it with You to atone for my sins

And to bring Your grace to souls in need.

Calm my fears; increase my trust.

May I gladly accept Your holy will and become more like You in trial.

If it be Your will, restore me to health so that I may work for Your honor and glory and the salvation of all men. *Amen.*

Mary, help of the sick, pray for me.

Prayer for the Sick

Dear Jesus, Divine Physician and Healer of the Sick, we turn to You in this time of illness. O dearest Comforter of the Troubled, alleviate our worry and sorrow with Your gentle love, and grant us the grace and strength to accept this burden. Dear God, we place our worries in Your hands. We place our sick under Your care and humbly ask that You restore Your servant to health again. Above all, grant us the grace to acknowledge Your holy will and know that whatsoever You do, You do for the love of us.   *Amen.*

The Great Commandment

You shall love the Lord your God with your whole heart, and with your whole soul, and with all your mind.

This is the greatest and the first commandment.

And the second is like it: you shall love your neighbor as yourself.

Guardian Angel

Angel of God, My Guardian Dear, to whom His love commits me here, ever this day be at my side, to light and guard, to rule and guide.   *Amen.*

Prayer in Time of Suffering

Behold me, my beloved Jesus, weighed down under the burden of my trials and sufferings, I cast myself at Your feet, that You may renew my strength and my courage, while I rest here in Your Presence. Permit me to lay down my cross in Your Sacred Heart, for only Your infinite goodness can sustain me; only Your love can help me bear my cross; only Your powerful hand can lighten its weight. O Divine King, Jesus, whose heart is so compassionate to the afflicted, I wish to live in You; suffer and die in You. During my life be to me my model and my support; At the hour of my death, be my hope and my refuge. *Amen.*

To the Sorrowful Mother for the Church and the Pontiff

Most Holy Virgin and Mother, your soul was pierced by a sword of sorrow in the passion of your divine Son, and in His glorious resurrection, you were filled with unending joy in His triumph! Obtain for us who call upon you, to be such partakers in the adversities of holy Church and in the sorrows of the Sovereign Pontiff as to be found worthy to rejoice with them in the consolations for which we pray, in the charity and peace of the same Christ our Lord. *Amen.*

(From the Racccolta #251)

13

Prayer for the Dying

✠

Most Merciful Jesus, lover of souls, I pray You, by the agony of Your most Sacred Heart, and by the sorrows of Your Immaculate Mother, to wash in Your Most Precious Blood, the sinners of the world who are now in their agony, and who will die today.

Heart of Jesus, once in agony, have mercy on the dying.   *Amen.*

Prayer for the Souls in Purgatory

✠

O gentle Heart of Jesus, ever present in the Blessed Sacrament, ever consumed with burning love for the poor captive souls in Purgatory, have mercy on them.

Be not severe in Your judgments, but let some drops of Your Precious Blood fall upon the devouring flames.

And, Merciful Savior, send Your angels to conduct them to place of refreshment, light and peace.   *Amen.*

Prayer for a Family

✠

O dear Jesus,
    I humbly implore You to grant Your special graces to our family. May our home be the shrine of peace, purity, love, labor and faith. I beg You, dear Jesus, to protect and bless all of us, absent and present, living and dead.

O Mary,
    loving Mother of Jesus, and our Mother, pray to Jesus for our family, for all the families of the world, to guard the cradle of the newborn, the schools of the young and their vocations.

Blessed Saint Joseph,
    holy guardian of Jesus and Mary, assist us by your prayers in all the necessities of life. Ask of Jesus that special grace which He granted to you, to watch over our home at the pillow of the sick and the dying, so that with Mary and with you, heaven may find our family unbroken in the Sacred Heart of Jesus. *Amen.*

Prayer of Reparation
✠

Eternal Father, I offer Thee the Sacred Heart of
Jesus, with all Its love, all Its sufferings and
all Its merits;
To expiate all the sins I have committed this day,
and during all my life.
Glory be to the Father, etc.
To purify the good I have done in my poor way
this day, and during all my life.
Glory be to the Father, etc.
To make up for the good I ought to have done
and that I have neglected this day and during
all my life.
Glory be to the Father, etc.

Daily Prayer to the Sacred Heart
✠

Sacred Heart of Jesus today I wish to live in
You, in Your grace, in which I desire at all
costs to persevere.
Keep me from sin and strengthen my will by
helping me to keep watch over my senses, my
imagination, and my heart.
Help me to correct my faults which are the
source of sin.
I beg You to do this, O Jesus, through Mary,
Your Immaculate Mother.

Mary Stewart's Prayer

Keep us, O God, from all pettiness.

Let us be large in thought, in word, in deed.

Let us be done with fault-finding and leave off all
self-seeking.

May we put away all pretense and meet each
other face to face, without self pity and without prejudice.

May we never be hasty in judgment, and
always be generous.

Let us always take time for all things, and make
us to grow calm, serene and gentle.

Teach us to put into action our better impulses, to
be straightforward and unafraid.

Grant that we may realize that it is the little things
of life that create differences, that in the big
things of life, we are as one.

And, O Lord God, let us not forget to be kind! *Amen.*

Christianity

In the home it is kindness;

In the business it is honesty;

In society it is courtesy;

In work it is fairness;

Toward the unfortunate it is sympathy;

Toward the weak it is help;

Toward the wicked it is resistance;

Toward the strong it is trust;

Toward the penitent it is forgiveness;

Toward the successful it is congratulation;

And toward God it is reverence and obedience.

Prayer to the Holy Spirit

✠

Come, Holy Spirit,
    fill my heart with Your holy gifts.

Let my weakness be penetrated with Your
    strength this very day that I may fulfill all
    the duties of my state conscientiously, that
    I may do what is right and just.

Let my charity be such as to offend no one,
    and hurt no one's feelings; so generous as to
    pardon sincerely any wrong done to me.

Assist me, O Holy Spirit,
    in all my trials of life, enlighten me in my
    ignorance, advise me in my doubts,
    strengthen me in my weakness, help me in
    all my needs, protect me in temptations and
    console me in afflictions.

Graciously hear me, O Holy Spirit,
    and pour Your light into my heart, my soul,
    and my mind.

Assist me to live a holy life and to grow in
    goodness and grace. *Amen.*

Act of Faith
✠

O my God, I firmly believe that You are one
God in three divine Persons, Father, Son,
and Holy Spirit. I believe that Your divine
son became man, died for our sins, and that
He will come to judge the living and the
dead. I believe these and all the truths
which the holy Catholic Church teaches,
because You have revealed them, Who can
neither deceive nor be deceived.

Act of Hope
✠

O my God, relying on Your almighty power
and infinite mercy and promises, I hope to
obtain pardon of my sins, the help of Your
grace, and life everlasting through the merits of Jesus Christ, my Lord and Redeemer.

Act of Love
✠

O my God, I love You above all things, with
my whole heart and soul, because You are
all-good and worthy of all love. I love my
neighbor as myself for the love of You. I
forgive all who have injured me, and ask
pardon of all whom I have injured. *Amen.*

Prayer Before Confession

✠

Come Holy Spirit into my soul.
    Enlighten my mind that I may know the sins I ought to confess, and grant me Your grace to confess them fully, humbly and with contrite heart.

Help me to firmly resolve not to commit them again.

O Blessed Virgin, Mother of my Redeemer, mirror of innocence and sanctity, and refuge of penitent sinners, intercede for me through the Passion of Your Son, that I may obtain the grace to make a good confession.

All you blessed Angels and Saints of God, pray for me, a most miserable sinner, that I may repent from my evil ways, that my heart may henceforth be forever united with yours in eternal love. *Amen.*

An Act of Contrition

O my God, I am heartily sorry for having offended You. I detest all my sins because I dread the loss of heaven and the pains of hell.

But most of all because they offend You, my God, Who are all good and deserving of all my love.

I firmly resolve, with the help of Your grace to sin no more and to avoid the near occasions of sin. *Amen.*

The Ten Commandments
✠

1. I am the Lord your God; you shall not have strange gods before Me.
2. You shall not take the name of the Lord your God in vain.
3. Remember to keep holy the Lord's day.
4. Honor your father and your mother.
5. You shall not kill.
6. You shall not commit adultery.
7. You shall not steal.
8. You shall not bear false witness against your neighbor
9. You shall not covet your neighbor's wife.
10. You shall not covet your neighbor's goods.

Precepts of the Church
✠

1. Assist at Mass on Sundays and Holy Days of obligation.
2. Fast and abstain on the days appointed.
3. Confess your sins at least once a year.
4. Receive Holy Communion during the Easter time.
5. Contribute to the support of the Church.
6. Observe the laws of the Church concerning marriage.

Prayer for Faith
✠

Lord, I believe: I wish to believe in Thee.

Lord, let my faith be full and unreserved, and let it penetrate my thought, my way of judging Divine things and human things.

Lord, let my faith be joyful and give peace and gladness to my spirit, and dispose it for prayer with God and conversation with men, so that the inner bliss of its fortunate possession may shine forth in sacred and secular conversation.

Lord, let my faith be humble and not presume to be based on the experience of my thought and of my feeling; but let it surrender to the testimony of the Holy Spirit, and not have any better guarantee than in docility to Tradition and to the authority of the *magisterium* of Holy Church.   *Amen.*

Pope Paul VI

Prayer
✠

Dearest Lord, teach me to be generous: teach me to serve You as You deserve: to give and not to count the cost, to fight and not to heed the wounds, to toil and not so seek for rest, to labor and not to ask for reward save that of knowing I am doing Your will.

St. Ignatius Loyola

22

Prayer After Confession

✠

My dearest Jesus,

I have told all my sins to the best of my ability. I have sincerely tried to make a good confession and I know that You have forgiven me. Thank You dear Jesus!

Your divine heart is full of love and mercy for poor sinners. I love You dear Jesus; You are so good to me.

My loving Savior, I shall try to keep from sin and to love You more each day.

Dearest Mother Mary,

pray for me and help me to keep all of my promises. Protect me and do not let me fall back into sin.

Dear God,

help me to lead a good life. Without Your grace I can do nothing. *Amen.*

My Breastplate

Christ be with me, Christ within me,
Christ behind me, Christ before me,
Christ beside me, Christ to win me,
Christ to comfort and restore me,
Christ beneath me, Christ above me,
Christ in quiet, Christ in danger,
Christ in hearts of all that love me,
Christ in mouth of friend and stranger.

St. Patrick

Prayer Before a Crucifix

Look down upon me, good and gentle Jesus
while before Your face I humbly kneel and,
with burning soul, pray and beseech You to
fix deep in my heart lively sentiments of
faith, hope, and charity; true contrition for
my sins, and a firm purpose of amendment.

While I contemplate, with great love and ten-
der pity, Your five most precious wounds,
pondering over them within me and calling
to mind the words which David, Your
prophet, said of You my Jesus:

"They have pierced My hands and My feet,
they have numbered all My bones." *Amen.*

Spiritual Communion

_When unable to receive Holy Communion, it is a pious
practice to make a Spiritual Communion. Say the follow-
ing prayer of St. Francis:_

I believe that You, O Jesus, are in the most holy
Sacrament. I love You and desire You. Come
into my heart. I embrace You. Oh, never leave
me. May the burning and most sweet power of
Your love, O Lord Jesus Christ, I beseech You,
absorb my mind that I may die through love of
Your love, Who were graciously pleased to die
through love of my love.

Prayer Before Communion

Come, O blessed Savior, and nourish my soul with
heavenly Food, the Food which contains every
sweetness and every delight. Come, Bread of
Angels, and satisfy the hunger of my soul. Come,
glowing Furnace of Charity, and enkindle in my
heart the flame of divine love. Come, Light of the
World, and enlighten the darkness of my mind.
Come, King of Kings, and make me obedient to
Your holy will. Come, loving Savior, and make me
meek and humble. Come, Friend of the Sick, and
heal the infirmities of my body and the weakness of
my soul. Come, Good Shepherd, my God and my
All, and take me to Yourself.
O most holy Mother, Mary Immaculate, prepare my
heart to receive my Savior.

Prayer After Holy Communion

✠

Dear Lord, help me to remove from my mind every thought or opinion which You would not sanction, every feeling from my heart which You would not approve.

Grant that I may spend the hours of the day gladly working with You according to Your will.

Help me just for today and be with me in it. In the long hours of work, that I may not grow weary or slack in serving You.

In conversations, that they may not be to me occasions of uncharitableness.

In the day's worries and disappointments, that I may be patient with myself and with those around me.

In moments of fatigue and illness, that I may be mindful of others rather than of myself.

In temptations, that I may be generous and loyal, so that when the day is over I may lay it at Your feet, with its successes which are all Yours, and its failures which are all my own, and feel that life is real and peaceful, and blessed when spent with You as the Guest of my soul. *Amen*

Prayer to the Holy Trinity

✠

Glory be to the Father,
    Who by His almighty power and love creat-
    ed me, making me in the image and like-
    ness of God.

Glory be to the Son,
    Who by His Precious Blood delivered me
    from hell, and opened for me the gates of
    heaven.

Glory be to the Holy Spirit,
    Who has sanctified me in the sacrament of
    Baptism, and continues to sanctify me by the
    graces I receive daily from His bounty.

Glory be to the Three adorable Persons of the
    Holy Trinity, now and forever. *Amen.*

For the Helpless Unborn

✠

Heavenly Father, You create men in Your own
    image, and You desire that not even the least
    among us should perish. In Your love for us,
    You entrusted Your only Son to the holy Vir-
    gin Mary. Now, in Your love, protect against
    the wickedness of the devil, those little ones
    to whom You have given the gift of life.

Anima Christi

✠

Soul of Christ sanctify me;
Body of Christ save me;
Blood of Christ inebriate me;
Water from the side of Christ wash me;
Passion of Christ strengthen me.
O good Jesus hear me;
Within Your wounds hide me;
Never permit me to be separated from You;
From the evil one protect me,
At the hour of my death call me,
And bid me come to You
That with Your saints
I may praise You forever.   *Amen.*

St. Ignatius

Prayer

✠

O Sweet Jesus, I desire neither life, nor death,
but Your most holy will. You are the One, O
Lord, that I long for. If it be Your holy will
to have me die, receive my soul; and grant
that in You and with You, I may receive everlasting rest. If it be Your holy will to have me
live longer upon this earth, give me the grace
to amend the rest of my life, and with good
works to glorify Your Holy Name.   *Amen.*

The Divine Praises

Blessed be God.

Blessed be His Holy Name.

Blessed be Jesus Christ, true God and true man.

Blessed be the Name of Jesus.

Blessed be His Most Sacred Heart.

Blessed be His Most Precious Blood.

Blessed be Jesus in the Most Holy Sacrament of the Altar.

Blessed be the Holy Spirit, the Paraclete.

Blessed be the great Mother of God, Mary most holy.

Blessed be her holy and Immaculate Conception.

Blessed be her glorious Assumption.

Blessed be the name of Mary, Virgin and Mother.

Blessed be St. Joseph, her most chaste spouse.

Blessed be God in His angels and in His Saints.

May the heart of Jesus, in the Most Blessed Sacrament, be praised, adored, and loved with grateful affection, at every moment, in all the tabernacles of the world, even to the end of time. *Amen.*

An Evening Visit

✠

Be with us, Lord, tonight. Stay to adore and praise, and give thanks for us while we sleep; to draw down mercy and grace upon the world; to give strength to the suffering souls in purgatory in their long night of waiting.

Stay with us, to ward off the anger of God from our crowded cities with their dens of vice, their crimes that call to Heaven for vengeance.

Stay with us, to guard the innocent, to sustain the tempted, to raise the fallen, to curb the power of the evil one, to prevent sin.

Stay with us, to comfort the sorrowing, to bless the death-beds, to grant contrition to the dying, to receive into the arms of Your mercy the thousands that this night must come before You for judgment.

O Good Shepherd, stay with Your sheep. Secure them against the perils that beset them. Stay, above all, with the suffering and dying. Grant us a quiet night and a perfect end. Be our merciful Shepherd to the last, that without fear we may appear before You as our Judge.

Evening Prayer

✠

Watch, O Lord, with those who wake, or watch,
    or weep tonight, and give Your Angels and
    Saints charge over those who sleep.
Tend Your sick ones, O Lord Christ.
Rest Your weary ones,
Bless Your dying ones,
Soothe Your suffering ones,
Pity Your afflicted ones,
Shield Your joyous ones,
And all for Your love's sake.   *Amen.*
                    St. Augustine

Prayer to Saint Michael

✠

Saint Michael, the Archangel, defend us in
    battle; be our defense against the wicked-
    ness and snares of the devil. May God
    rebuke him, we humbly pray; and do you, O
    Prince of the heavenly host, by the power of
    God, thrust into hell Satan and the other evil
    spirits who prowl about the world for the
    ruin of souls.   *Amen.*

Most Sacred Heart of Jesus,
Have mercy on us. *(Three times.)*

Anonymous

✠

I asked God for strength,
that I might achieve...

I was made weak,
that I might learn humbly to obey.

I asked for health,
that I might do greater things...

I was given infirmity,
that I might do better things.

I asked for riches,
that I might be happy...

I was given poverty,
that I might be wise.

I asked for power,
that I might have the praise of men...

I was given weakness,
that I might feel the need of God.

I asked for all things,
that I might enjoy life...

I was given life,
that I might enjoy all things.

I got nothing that I asked for,
but everything I had hoped for.

Almost despite myself,
my unspoken prayers were answered.

I am among all men, most richly blessed!